For Talia and Joseph – J.Z.
To Geoffrey and Audrey – J.B.C.

First edition for the United States, Canada, and the Philippines published 2002
by Barron's Educational Series, Inc.

Eight Candles to Light copyright © Frances Lincoln Limited 2002
Text copyright © Jonny Zucker 2002
Illustrations copyright © Jan Barger Cohen 2002

First published in Great Britain in 2002 by
Frances Lincoln Limited, 4 Torriano Mews,
Torriano Avenue, London NW5 2RZ

All inquiries should be addressed to:
Barron's Educational Series, Inc.
250 Wireless Boulevard
Hauppauge, New York 11788
http://www.barronseduc.com

Library of Congress Catalog Card No.: 2001099794
International Standard Book No.: 0-7641-2266-5

Printed in Singapore
9876543

FESTIVAL TIME!

Eight Candles To Light

A Chanukah Story

Jonny Zucker

Illustrated by Jan Barger Cohen

BARRON'S

It's Chanukah. On the first night
we light one candle.
We listen to the amazing
story of Judah Maccabee.

We fry latkes in oil. They sizzle and spit in the pan! These potato pancakes taste so good!

I love playing spinning
games with the dreidel.

We sing songs about the brave Maccabees and the cruel King Antiochus.

We all give each other
presents in colorful wrappings.

My family sits around the
table and enjoys a festive meal.

On the last night,
we light eight candles
to remind us of the
miracle of Chanukah—
our festival of light.

The Story of Chanukah

More than 2,100 years ago, the Syrian king Antiochus IV wanted to make the Jews worship many gods, like all the other people in his empire. The Jews refused to pray to any but the one true God. Antiochus punished them by taking over the Holy Temple and destroying the sacred scrolls of the Law (the **Torah**). Many Jews were killed for refusing to bow down to the pagan gods.

In Modi'in, a town between Jerusalem and the sea, a Jewish priest named Mattathias lived with his five sons. When a Syrian official tried to force the Jewish people to worship the pagan gods, Mattathias refused and killed the official. He and his sons and many other Jewish families fled to the hills, where they could hide from Antiochus' soldiers and fight against them.

Led by Mattathias' eldest son, Judah Maccabee, the Jews fought for three years and defeated Antiochus' army. They then returned to the Temple in Jerusalem. They wanted to relight the sacred **menorah** – a seven-branched candlestick – but there was only enough oil to keep it lit for one day, and they knew it would take eight days to get more oil. But a miracle happened: The oil kept burning for eight days and nights.

In memory of the miracle and the victory, Jewish people today light an eight-branched **menorah,** called a hanukkiyah, at Chanukah.

One candle – the **shamash** or "helper" – is used to light the others. One candle is lit on the first evening, two on the second evening, until the eighth evening when eight candles are lit. These candles remind everyone how the oil in the Temple lasted for eight days.

During the festival, Jewish people sing special songs and give each other money and presents. To remind them of the miracle of the oil, they also eat **latkes** (potato cakes) and doughnuts, which are both fried in oil.

Children play games with spinning tops called **dreidels**. Each of the four faces of a **dreidel** has a Hebrew letter: **nun, gimmel, hey, and shin**. When put together, they represent the phrase:

Nes gadol hayah sham – a great miracle happened there.

20